I0022445

Adeline Dutton Train Whitney, Adeline Dutton Train Whitney

Bird Talk

A Calendar of the Orchard and Wild Wood

Adeline Dutton Train Whitney, Adeline Dutton Train Whitney

Bird Talk
A Calendar of the Orchard and Wild Wood

ISBN/EAN: 9783744661546

Printed in Europe, USA, Canada, Australia, Japan

Cover: Foto ©Andreas Hilbeck / pixelio.de

More available books at **www.hansebooks.com**

BIRD-TALK

A CALENDAR OF THE ORCHARD AND WILD-WOOD

BY

ADELINE D. T. WHITNEY

BOSTON AND NEW YORK
HOUGHTON, MIFFLIN AND COMPANY
The Riverside Press, Cambridge
1887

Copyright, 1887,

ADELINE D. T. WHITNEY AND HOUGHTON, MIFFLIN & CO.

All rights reserved.

The Riverside Press, Cambridge:
Electrotyped and Printed by H. O. Houghton & Co.

CONTENTS.

CONTENTS.

I.

January.

IN THE EVERGREENS.
(*The Chickadees.*)

THE Norway spruces, grand and old,
Stretching their green arms manifold,
With cone-hung fingers reach awide
To drop their wealth on every side,
As noble hearts whose secret strength
Issues in broadcast good at length.

Stately straight, like masts of ships,
From bases huge to rocket-tips,
Lift the single-purposed stems ;
Great, low branches, with their hems
Fringed and fragrant, sweep the sward ;
Lesser levels heavenward

Build their floorings — all the way
Thick their spiny carpets lay
Over each circumference
In a dull magnificence.

Living hearts and homes of life :
Warm and hushed from tempest-strife
In deep shelter ; vast abroad
Like the inviting grace of God,
Waiting, welcoming.   Only this
Rears their verdant palaces !
Grace for what ?   And home for whom ?
Filled with summer's high perfume,
Rich with granaries of seed
Stored against long wintry need, —

Ample spaces, sweetly hid,
Chambers of a pyramid —
With what occupancy, say,
Are ye all alive to-day ?

" We," reply the mighty trees,
" Have grown to hold the Chickadees ! "
        .   .   .   .   .   .
        " Chick-adee — dee — dee,"
          Sing the little birds with glee.
        " Don't you see — don't you see
            How it would be
            With such as we,
      Except each free and gracious tree
            Were built and spread,
            From root to head,
            That we might fed
      And sheltered be — be — be ?

" Chickadee, dee — dee — dee !
God made and waited for the tree
Before He made the chickadee !
Chickadee-dee — Chickadee-dee —
   Chickadee, dee — dee — dee ! "

II.

𝔉𝔢𝔟𝔯𝔲𝔞𝔯𝔭.

IN THE THORN-THICKET.

(*The Blue Jay.*)

SOMETHING glorious, something gay,
    Flits and flashes this-a-way!
Thwart the hemlock's dusky shade,
Rich in color full displayed,
    Swiftly vivid as a flame —
Blue as heaven, and white as snow —
Doth the lovely creature go.
    What may be his dainty name?

"Only this" — the people say —
"Saucy, chattering, scolding Jay!"

Cruel, teasing, malapert —
Mocking taunt or mortal hurt
Hurling at some lesser one,
Reckoning it for life and fun —
Fierce and cowardly — oh, pray,
Who would be a splendid Jay?

Are you wondering wherefore so
In heaven's livery he should go?
Maybe Heaven would have you know
Livery is not birthright, dear,
And color is not character.

Hear the mean and bitter note
Coming from his banded throat!
Eager scorn and jealous blame
For fault where he is just the same;
  Quick accusal, close akin
  To crookedness of inward sin!—
Ah, He who set the mark on Cain
Still somewhere makes the witness plain!
Then let him go his glittering way;
Let him shine on, as shine he may—
Fair-plumed, fine-crowned, false-hearted Jay!

  . . . .

    "Say, say, say!
     So, so, so!
Did you see, did you see
    Cousin Crow—ho, ho!
Where did he, where did he,
    Where did he go?
     D' ye know?
He 's a quack, quack, quack,
With his clack, clack, clack!
  He 's a villain, he 's a villain,
And he 's black, black, black!

    "Stay, stay, stay!
    Whatsay, whatsay?—
     Then ye know

I 'm a crow?
'Even though bedizened so ' —
Hee, hee, ho!
'That 's the way,' d' ye say,
'Tongues betray' ?
Well, really — well, really! —
Whatsay, whatsay, whatsay ?
'Inside just as black ' ? —
Good lack! good lack! good lack!"
. . . .

Something ugly — something ill,
Flees off, jeering, jabbering still.

III.

March.

ON THE BARE BOUGH.

(The Song Sparrow.)

THE careful winter was hardly gone,
And the careful spring was coming on :
So much to manage, so much to make —
So many matters to undertake —
It seemed to me that I had to do
More than ever I could get through.

But, walking along by the orchard wall,
Where the sopsyvines in autumn fall,
On a rough bare apple-bough overhead
Lit a little sparrow, and this he said —
Telling of all *he* found to do
With a thankful gladness that thrilled me through :

. . . .

        " Sweet — sweet —
          Sweet — sweet !
    Chipper, chipper, chipper, chipper, — chip !

Oh what a merry, merry, busy, busy thing Life is!
Sweet — sweet —
Sweet — sweet!
Hurry, hurry, hurry, hurry — quick, quick, quick!
There was never, never, such a busy time as this!
The world to wake!
And the nests to make!
Sweet — sweet!
Yes, yes, yes, yes, yes, yes,
We're all busy — God's busy,
God's happy — we're all happy,
For we're His!"

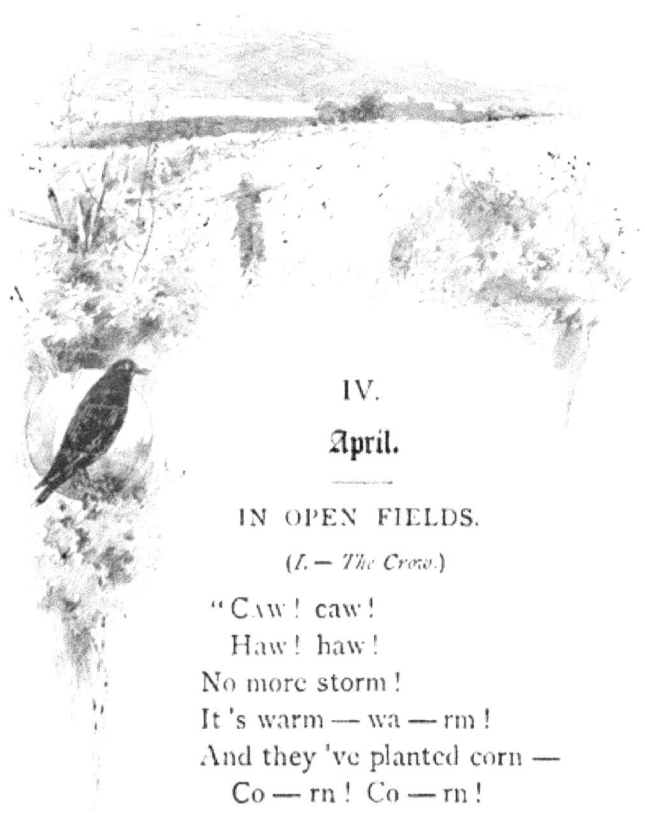

IV.

April.

IN OPEN FIELDS.

(I. — The Crow.)

"Caw! caw!
 Haw! haw!
No more storm!
It's warm — wa — rm!
And they've planted corn —
 Co — rn! Co — rn!
 Come on, come on!
 The farmer's gone!
His man of straw
I scorn — sco — rn!
 Because — cau — se!
 I knew what 't was
  Soon's I sa — w!
  Haw! ha — w!
I've stolen corn
Before he was bo — rn!
 Haw! Ha — w!"

(*II. — The Robin.*)

" Chee — er up, chee — er up, I 'm he — re !
 I 'm he — re, and I 've come to stay !
 It 's the bravest time of the ye — ar —
 Chee — er up, chee — er up, I say !

" The sno — ws are over and go — ne,
 Ru — n and rippled awa — y ;
 The lo — ng, long summer's begu — n,
 And the wo — rld is going to be ga — y !

" Now and then there may be, to be su — re,
 A clou — dy or rainy day ;
 But they never come to endu — re —
 Chee — er up, chee — er up, anyway !

" Chee — er up, chee — er up, I 'm he — re,
 With a thou — w — sand things to sa — y ;
 It 's the swe — et, sweet spring of the ye — ar —
 Chee — er up, chee — er up right awa — y !"

V.

May.

HID IN THE LILAC.

(The Catbird.)

Close by my window there runs a fence,
  Picketed white and evenly ;
And over its corner, in opulence,
  Tumble the heaps of a lilac-tree,
That reach and broaden, and loftier rear,
Growing and thickening, year by year.

Mystical depths of quiet shade ;
  Fairy splendors of emerald sheen ;
Mimic chamber and colonnade
  Shaped by the boughs and bountiful green.
Oh wonderful world that I cannot see
Hid in the heart of the lilac-tree !

I watched the leaf-gates where light crept in
  A little space, as the sunshine played —
And the breath of the breeze did further win —
  And wished for the moment that I were made

So light and tiny that I might push
My way to the heart of a lilac bush !

The thought took form with the longing ; down
To the line that the square-topped pickets run
Straight under the lilac's massy crown,
Swept a little bird ; and I saw it done.
As best and only the thing could be,
That which I wanted was done for me.

Pausing and glancing, with shy demurs,
Warily hopping from pale to pale,
Setting those dainty small feet of hers
On point by point of the trestle-rail,
A black-winged catbird with soft gray breast
Ran in to the covert that hid her nest.

" Ah, now," I said, " there 'll be life and fun !
I 've got a neighbor : and well I know
She 'll be a blithe and talkative one ;
To see her come and to see her go,
Over the causeway she finds so pat
To her little purpose — there 's sport in that !

" And then the interests I shall share —
Love-chat and confab, snip-snap and all —
Household counsel, and gossip of air,
Without the trouble of going to call ! "
I longed for the eaves-dropping to begin :
How glad I was they were moving in !

But I never knew till I came to try,
Listening curious, day by day,

Now to an argument, now to a cry,
  How much a catbird could have to say :
Nor half how human the tale could be
Told in trills from a lilac-tree.

        .   .   .   .   .

      "Oh, I 'm a 'catbird' ?
        ' With a temper,' — yes !
          Pretty good !
      Yet I 'm not amiss,
        I 'm not a bad bird,
          If I 'm understood !

      " It 's only that word —
        The only bad word
          I ever say,
And that on a very bad, provoking day,
When the world works some mean old horrid way !
          ' Ye — a — ow !
            I sw — ow !'

      " Or when I 'm flurried
        And over-worried,
          Doing my best
          About my nest,
And things go criss-cross — oh, you all know how they
      do !
        Then I express it —
        For I can't repress it
Any more than you can, and I wa — il out — just like
      you —
          ' Mi — eu !
            Mi — e — ux !'

" French for ' better ! '
(With a silent letter)
Rhymes to other things the French say, too :
Oh, puss and I — we know a thing or two !
    But it is n't swearing,
    Nor yet despairing ;
We only want — the ' luck of next time ' — so we do !
    It is n't fret and fuss,
    Nor any petty muss —
We 're never clamorous, nor too impetuous,
    But the world 's in debt to us :
    If we don't see to it,
    Who will take heed to it ?
Pay up, pay up, old world, your I O U ! "

ON A GRASS-HEAD.

(*The Bobolink.*)

" I 'm Bob-o-link !
    Bob-o-link !
Here and there,
Quick as a wink,
Before you can think —
    Think ! Think !
That 's Bobolink !

" Lady Link ! Lady Link !
Follow, follow, follow —
Follow me, Lady Link !
Don't stop to prink —
    Prink ! Prink !

" The world 's in a hurry —
   A blessed pucker and flurry —
      For life is short,
   And the summer 's begun,
      And there 's naught, naught, naught,
   But loving and thanksgiving to be done
   Under the glad, glad, loving, loving Sun !
      That 's what I say —
         And think !
      Bob-o-link !   Bob-o-link !   Bob-o-link !

" That 's why I 'm here !
      Black-coated,
      White-cravatted,
         Bob-o-link !
   Don't you see ?
      Did n't you think ?
   Preaching Gospel every year —
      Bob-o-link ! "

VI.
June.

IN THE ASH-TREE.

(*The Vireos.*)

An old, old tree with a mighty shade —
   Seamed and rifted in limb and trunk
With lines and gullies that years have made
   And frosts and tempests have worn and sunk —
Shelters me where I sit to-day,
   Hearing the laughter of leaves at play,
And the slow-swayed branches' gentle moan
Admonishing in grave undertone.

Like orchestral accompaniment,
   Across whose diapason low
A voice in slender sweetness sent
   Runs with ripples that come and go,
Are the sober symphonies of the tree
   To the small bird-warble that pleases me
With its one refrain and repeat alway,
   And the self-same story it has to say :

" Little witch, little witch !
   Oh, there you be !
Look up quick
   And listen to me !
There you sit
   In the old ash-tree.

" Little witch, little witch,
   Turn round to me.
The light is rich
   And the air is free ;
Oh, what a bliss
   It is to be !
Sweet little witch !
   Do you love me ? "

" And what if I did ? "
   " Why, then 't would be
Per — fectly jolly
   For you and me !
We 'd set up a house
   Right off, you see ! "

" Let me consider " —
   "Oh, yes, indeed ;
To make you consider
   Is all I need !"

She had n't considered for half a wink
When he was back again :

   " What do you think ?
Here is a twig, dear ;

Shall we build ?
Little witch, little witch,
  I 'm sure you 're skilled !
I'll bring you sticks,
  And leaves, and grass,
And you shall fix
  For yourself, sweet lass !
You shall have your will —
  I 'll do as you bid —
And I 'll keep quite still " —
  " Oh, I wish you did ! "

He hushed his voice to a plaintive trill,
But under his breath it quivered still :

  " Little witch, little witch,
    I love — you so ;
  Maybe — more
    Than you wish — to know ! "

Then low she twittered :

  " That 's dif — ferent !
    Why did n't you — tell me
  What you — meant ?
    You love — me — much —
  And *you* love — me — more —
    Why did n't you say it
      So before ? "

Ah, then there was chatter — then there was glee :
And the honeymoon sped right merrily.
I heard it all 'neath the old ash-tree ;
It was *so* like other folks' ways, you see !

UNDER THE LAUREL BUSH.

(The Oven-Bird.)

Among the pines I heard this little song ;
I heard it all the Sunday morning long :
The hymn-tune of the Golden-crowned Thrush —
A voice — as flame was sight, once — from the bush !

Just one clear call, and then a thrill of sound
Flung all its wavering ecstasy around ;
A melody with wings that beat the air
Till a swift sweetness trembled everywhere.

One can but think it : it was passing fine
For clumsy syllables of yours and mine :
In hurried utterance when I strive to say
What it was like, words stumble on the way :

.   .   .   .

" Oh, I shi — ver, iver, iver, iver, iver, —
Oh, I qui — ver, iver, iver, iver, iver, —
With the bliss, bliss, bliss, bliss, bliss
Of a happy day like this, this, this !

" Oh, what a riv — er, iver, iver, iver, iver
Of rapture runs forever, ever, ever
From the Bosom of the Best, Best, Best,
Down into every little nest, nest, nest !
   Hallelu — jah, lujah, lujah, lujah, lujah,
   Amen — amen — amen, men, men ! "

VII.

July.

IN THE CHERRY-TREES.
(*Tanager.*)

Chip chur — r — r !
I 'm the cherry-eater — r — r, —
 The Tanager !
  Do you demur — r — r ?

Chip, chip, chur — r — r !
Is n't it wor — r — th
 A cherry or mor — r — e
 Out of such a stor — r — e,
  To see me, sir — r — r ?
   I 'm the Tanager — r — r !

Please, may I per — r — ch ?
 If you will not stir — r — r,
Nor watch me too particu — ler — r — r,
You shall not be wor — r — se
 By little me
 For your char — r — i — ty !
Nor left in the lur — r — ch
 With an empty tree !

Don't you go to chur — r — ch,
 I wonder, sir — r — r ?
 Does n't it occur — r — r
  To you instantly
  What a chance 't would be
To mind what the ministers always pr — r — each, —
Up to the golden rule to r — r — each —
And do as you 'd be done by to me ?
  Tut, tut, good sir — r — r !
  You 're a wor — r — ship — er—r — r !
  I 'm only, — chip, chur — r — r, —
An ignorant little red Tanager !

IN THE BIRCH HOLLOW.

(*Savanna Sparrow.*)

A sweet-breathed pine, and an old oak-tree
Hold the cords of my hammock for me.
Over me as I lazily lie,
Sapphire glints from a crystal sky
Set with the leaves' soft emerald seem
Like the palace roof of a fairy dream ;
Or the builded glories beheld by them
Who walk in the New Jerusalem.

A meadow-open spreads fair and low
Beyond, where the golden daisies blow :
And farther yet, in a stillness deep,
The dusky lines of the woodland sweep.
But half the hollow that dips between
With twinkling birches is glittering green,
Whose bright-massed tops in the sunshine make
Sparkle and shimmer as of a lake.

Scents of the bay and fern and pine
Richly visit this nook of mine ;
The air in whose warmth their odors seethe
Is blessedness only just to breathe ;
And the stillness of all things, far and near,
Is deeper beatitude to hear ;
Till the hushed repose with a note is broken
Sweeter than silence, — like silence spoken.

In the little birch-vale, where the shadow hides
His nest, the savanna sparrow bides ;
And when other singers are idly still
His small, soft chitter drifts up the hill,
Bearing the message that he has found,
And chirps as he sits there on the ground,
For the heart-content that interpreteth
The wee, wee word that the sparrow saith : —

Sip, sip, sip, —
Ever so little, —
If ever so little — sip !
Sip, sip, sip,
Of the life that's a lift !
Sip, sip, sip !
We can take but a little, — a little, —
Of the life that 's a gift !
But it 's here, — it 's here, — sip, sip !
It 's here, and it 's free !
We can get
But a bit ;
Yet if ever so little, — so little, —
Sip, sip, — sip, sip, — sip, sip !
It 's for you and for me, —

Sip, sip, —
The life that is free!

Sip, sip, — sip, sip, — sip, sip!
Ever so little, — so little, —
Ever so little, — sip!
It's here, — it's free, — it's a gift!
Sip, sip, — sip, sip, — sip, sip,
Of the life that's a lift!

VIII.

August.

IN DEEP WOODS

(*The Least Pewee.*)

THE least pewee of all,
  He sits and sings
As do the human small,
  Impertinent things
    Among the rest,
    Checking the best ;
   One single, urgent note
    From his intrusive throat —
Two-syllabled, if that count anything —
Making the sweet woods suddenly to ring,
As if his realm, prone to his tiny will :
"Shut up ! Shut up ! Be still, be still, be still ! "
    In early twilight time,
    When the long ridge I climb,
     And cross the crown,
   To where the deepening glades
   Of holy forest shades
    Shut in and down ;

And the fine, far-off, tender gloom
Makes sacred, separate place and room
Where the hermit-thrush, like a bird of prayer, abides
And tunes his psalm for morn and evening-tides, —
    I hold my breath
    For what he uttereth,
And the hushed air is cloven with the first
Pure calm of sound — then comes, with hurried burst,
Like cheap, mean interference of the world
With willing thoughts of worship — strangely hurled
    Upon the soul of me
    In taunt and mockery —
The little insolence of the Least Pewee,
Quenching the rare, with commonplace to fill :
" Shut up! shut up! shut up! Be still ! Be still !"

(*The Hermit-Thrush.*)

"Oh, here dwell we,
  So qui-etly, —
    Faith-fully !
     Lone-lily ?
      Ah, very true, very true !
       Yet — if — you knew !
I *tell* you — I *tell* you — I *tell* you —
   That if — you knew —
  Ah *if* you — *if* you knew !

" Though far — and deep
  The shad-ows creep,
    Yet heav-en — is blue,
    And shi-ning, shi-ning through,

Forev-er, ev-er true !
I *tell* you — I *tell* you — I *tell* you,
For-ev-er true !

" On-ly a few —
A ver-y few,
Who ev-er knew
What *I* tell you!
I *tell* you — I *tell* you — I *tell* you —
Ah, *if* you knew !
Ah, *if* you, *if* you knew !

" Oh, did — you — could — you see
What comes — what comes — to me !
Oh will you — oh will you — oh will you
But wait — with me —
And list — with me —
And look — with me ?
I *tell* you — I *tell* you — I *tell* you
The things — that be
Are ver-ily
More than — more than — you see !

" Oh listen, oh listen, oh listen !
For if — for if — you knew
The peace — the peace — I do !
I *tell* you — I *tell* you — I *tell* you
The tru-th is tru-e !
The tru-th, the tru-th, is tru-e ! "

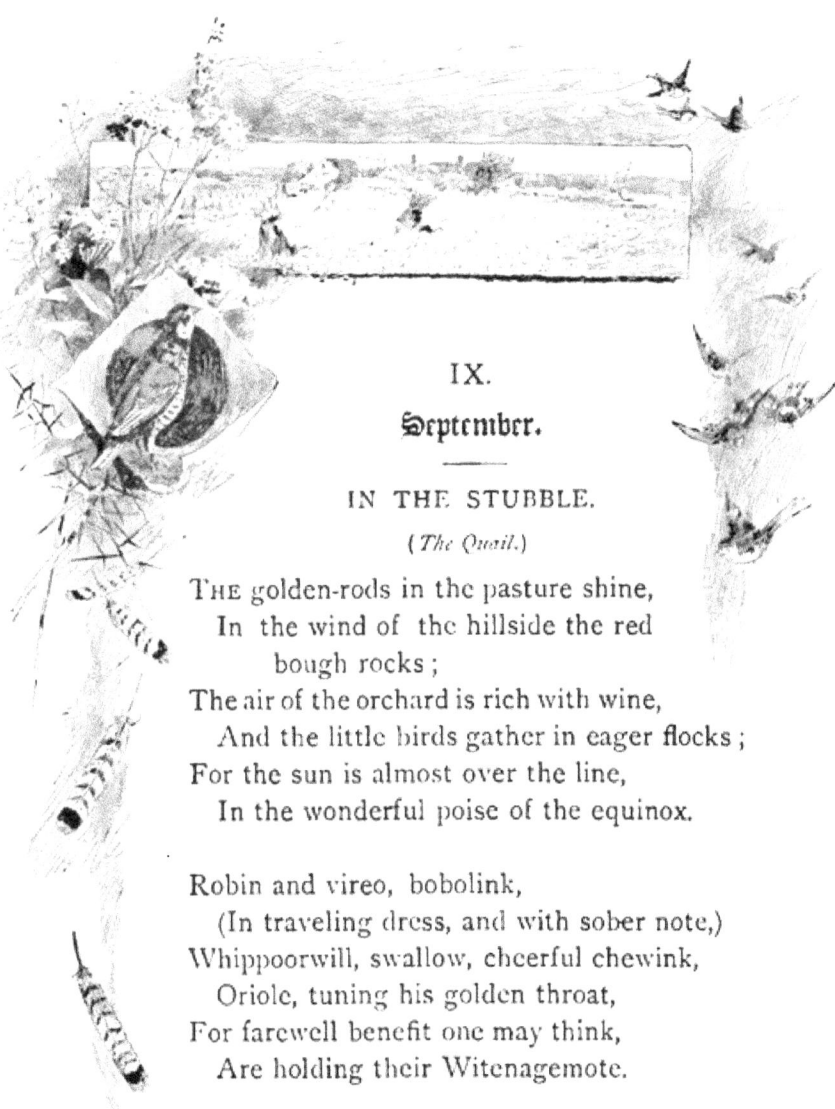

IX.

September.

IN THE STUBBLE.

(*The Quail.*)

THE golden-rods in the pasture shine,
   In the wind of the hillside the red
      bough rocks ;
The air of the orchard is rich with wine,
   And the little birds gather in eager flocks ;
For the sun is almost over the line,
   In the wonderful poise of the equinox.

Robin and vireo, bobolink,
   (In traveling dress, and with sober note,)
Whippoorwill, swallow, cheerful chewink,
   Oriole, tuning his golden throat,
For farewell benefit one may think,
   Are holding their Witenagemote.

Gay and noisy, or tenderly glad,
   Gathers each family and clan,
Telling what beautiful times they 've had,
   Repeating the summer as well as they can ;

Till one almost cries out, vexed and sad,
  Birds have the best of it, over man!

But down in the gentle intervale
  That the feeding life of the hills receives, —
Roughened now with the stubble pale
  Where the farmer gathered his mighty sheaves —
Runs the shy brown-breasted quail,
  Gleaning the sweetness the harvest leaves.

He cannot fly, any more than we,
  Away from the winter's cold and threat,
To sunny fields by the southern sea,
  A cheap new holiday to get.
He must bear, and bide, and patient be
  For the blithe, brave summer that 's coming yet!

And I think, as he walks in the golden light
  Of the equal day and his own content,
While the quick-winged singers are thronging bright
  Overhead in their busy parliament,
If he does n't say it at least he might,
  The word that his spring song really meant:

Morc yet!   More yet!   More yet!
    Not over quite, not quite!
        All right!
  Not yet — doth God — forget!
  More love, — more life — more light!
        All right!

X.

October.

AMONG FALLING LEAVES.

(*The Tree-Sparrow.*)

Theme : " Whee-hee-hö-hee !"

THE leaves are ripe; earth everywhere
 Is gorgeous with their color-stain ;
A glory streams through all the air ;
 Like light in church through tinted
   pane,
    That shimmers slowly.

The anxious time for nesting bird
 And toiling man is over now ;
Only some casual song is heard,
 Or easy whistle at the plough
    Of yeoman lowly.

It is the time of quiet earned ;
 The Sabbath of stern labor won ;

Hallowed since first the planets burned —
  The seventh-day calm of the well-done ;
    And it is holy.

I hear a small, sweet strain that floats
  Among the tree-tops of October,
Seeming to say, in gentle notes,
  So few, so clear, so softly sober —
    " Oh, *keep* — it ho-ly ! "

The little sparrow of the north
  Comes when the leaves and nuts are dropping,
And on the stillness warbles forth
  This message, in his long flight stopping —
    " Yes — *keep* — it ho-ly ! "

Dear word — yet now, as long ago,
  The " wherefore " of six days' pursuing !
God's Sabbath is but builded so,
  And only grows of urgent doing.
    "Keep — the week — ho-ly ! "

XI.

November.

IN THE EARLY SNOW.

(*The Goldfinch.*)

A soft white sprinkle on the pasture lies;
   The hemlock tips are turned to ostrich plumes;
And seen against the clear blue of the skies,
   The orchard boughs look full of apple-blooms.

Where the sun slants along the forest side,
   Making the calm November afternoon
Like a faint lingering of the summer tide,
   A flock of finches pipes in cheery tune.

In undress uniform; the gaudy gold
   Of the parade-day thriftily put by.
Life has grown serious; with storm and cold
   And gray cloud banners, winter marches nigh.

But "Who's afraid?" their quick call seems to cry.
   "Not me — not me — not me " — comes answer-
      ing clear

From brave, sweet throats that valiantly defy
  The changing humors of a hemisphere.

" We 'll-see — we 'll-see — we 'll-see " — it sounds again ;
  Till, listening closer, I interpret more,
And the small syllables make full and plain
  A larger meaning than they held before.

" We 're-wee — we 're-wee — indeed, indeed, — we 're-
      wee ;
  Yet we — can sing — we still, we still, can sing ;
The winter 's chill — chill, chill as it can be ;
  But He, yes, He — will see — to everything ! "

XII.

December.

FROM THE OLD BARN GABLE.

(Screech-Owl.)

So much in the world, and I don't know whoo — oo-oo,
  oo-oo — se !
  So much to get, and I don't know how, — ow-ow, ow-
    ow, oo — w !
I wonder if I can ever choo — oo-oo, oo-oo, oo — se
  To be anything better than I am no — w, ow-ow, ow-
    ow, o — ow !

What good are my great big half-blind ey — ey-ey, ey-ey,
  ey — es,
  That search for all, and can nothing see — ee-ee-ee-ee ?
Why did they make me so stupid — wi — i-i, i-i, i — se,
  Oh, *why* did they make a foo — l of me — ee-ee-ee-ee ?

I wonder if anywhere befo — o-o-o-o-ore
  I 've been, and missed, and lost, till no — w, ow-ow, ow-
    ow, o — w

I shall have to be forever mo — o-o, o-o, o — re
   I don't know what, and I don't know ho — w, o v-ow,
     ow-ow, o — w ?

What's that the little children sa — a-a, a-a, a — y,
  . There in the light, where they trim their tree — ee-ee,
    ee-ee, ee,
The glorious light in which they pla — a-a, a-a, a — y,
   And that only blinds and tortures me — ee-ee, ee-ee, ee ?

" It was ever ever, so long ago — o-o, o-o, o — o,
   The blessed Christ was born to-da — a-a, a-a, a — y,
And helpless laid in a manger lo — o-o, o-o, o — w : "
   Is that what the little children sa — a-a, a-a, a — y ?

I don't know why they are singing so — o-o, o-o, o,
   And I don't know what the Christ may be — e-e, e-e, ee,
But I wish that now, or long ago — o-o o-o, o — o,
   Or ever, some Christ would come to me — e-e, e-e, ee !

  .   ·   ·   ·   ·   ·   ·   ·   ·   ·

    The screech-owl sat in the gable cold,
      And blinked his big eyes mournfully ;
    But what if the word which came of old
      Hath message for him, as for you and me ?

    If some time, Love, with its wonderful reach
      Down the whole creation that doth complain,
    Shall redeem the owls, and sublimely teach
      How none may cry for a soul in vain ?

MRS. WHITNEY'S BOOKS.

Faith Gartney's Girlhood. $1.50.

If there is any other American writer who so thoroughly understands girls as Mrs. Whitney, we have yet to see the evidence of his or her knowledge. She writes as if the experiences of her own youth were as fresh in her mind as if that time were only yesterday. — *The Literary World.*

Hitherto: A Story of Yesterdays. $1.50.

Mrs. Whitney always writes with a purpose; and her words go right down to the innermost soul of all earnest readers. . . . Her stories are of the highest and best order of fiction. — *Louisville Courier-Journal.*

Patience Strong's Outings. $1.50.

A charming story for girls, teaching in the most engaging manner some of the most important lessons of life, yet mingling the story and the lesson so skillfully and with so much humor as to lure the reader on with the most beneficent fascination.

The Gayworthy's: A Story of Threads and Thrums. $1.50.

Accompanying a rare sympathetic comprehension of her subject, there is an air of purity and refinement surrounding all Mrs. Whitney writes, that we have not detected in any other writer for the young. — *The Literary World.*

A Summer in Leslie Goldthwaite's Life. Illustrated. $1.50.

This is a lovely story, full of sweet and tender feeling, kindly Christian philosophy, and noble teaching. It is pleasantly spiced, too, with quaint New England characters, and their odd, shrewd reflections. — GRACE GREENWOOD.

Real Folks. Illustrated. $1.50.

We place this book first in the list of those sure to interest girls just becoming women; and we take pleasure in recommending it. — *Louisville Courier-Journal.*

We Girls: A Home Story. Illustrated. $1.50.

Who that was introduced to Leslie Goldthwaite, that charming summer among the White Mountains, will not gladly seize the opportunity of renewing the acquaintance as she takes her place with "We Girls." — *Christian Register* (Boston).

The Other Girls. Illustrated. $1.50.

Of all the conceptions of young womanhood which fiction has given us, we know of few so natural and lovable as Bel Bree — *Boston Journal.*

Sights and Insights: Patience Strong's Story of Over the Way. 2 volumes. $3.00.

One would suppose that nothing new could be said about the Alps, St. Peter's, the Pantheon, Westminster Abbey, or a score of other things, which every traveler sees, and every traveler writes about; but Mrs. Whitney has invested each and all with a charm and freshness that make them seem like revelations of new realities. — *Boston Transcript.*

Odd or Even. $1.50.

Mrs. Whitney is one of America's best story-tellers. Her writings are pure, bright, entertaining, and improving. Her present book, " Odd, or Even," is one of her best — sweet, tender, and humorous throughout. — *Episcopal Register* (Philadelphia).

Bonnyborough. $1.50.

This is a New England story in scene and characters, possessing the earnestness, the nobility of air and spirit, and the interest which characterizes all that Mrs. Whitney writes.

Homespun Yarns. Containing "Zerub Throop's Experiment," " Buttered Crusts," " My Mother Put It On," " Girl Noblesse," "The Little Savages of Beetle Rock," and other Short Stories. $1.50.

Boys at Chequasset. $1.50.

Mrs. Whitney is the author of a number of books for girls which are unique for simple, practical wisdom. . . . In the little book now published she shows that she can write for boys with much of the skill that was peculiar to Jacob Abbott. — *Christian Intelligencer* (New York).

Mother Goose for Grown Folks. New Edition, enlarged. Illustrated by HOPPIN. $1.50.

Fancy a poetical key to Mother Goose! But no one must read it as a study. It is too delightful for that. Any one may read it, however, for its freshness, humor, delicacy, and cleverness. — *Quebec Chronicle*.

Just How: A Key to the Cook-Books. $1.00.

A person entirely ignorant of cooking could, it seems to us, go into her kitchen with this book in her hand, and be confident of success in all the simple forms of cooking. It is not possible to speak too strongly in praise of the peculiar method and methods of the book. — H. H., *in Denver Tribune*.

Holy Tides. Square 16mo, beautifully printed and bound, 75 cents.

A tasteful book of thoughtful poetry; devoted to Advent, Christmas, Epiphany, Lent, Whitsunday, Trinity, and Easter.

Pansies. A Volume of Poems. 16mo, $1.25.

A book which is singularly free from artistic commonplace, and everywhere breathes a spirit of refined fancy and thoughtful earnestness which should commend it to all true sympathies, even if it were not matched by so rare a degree of poetical merit. — *New York Tribune*.

Daffodils. 16mo, gilt top, $1.25.

A very attractive book, containing the poems written by Mrs. Whitney during several years past.

*** *For sale by all Booksellers. Sent by mail, post-paid, on receipt of price by the Publishers,*

HOUGHTON, MIFFLIN & CO., BOSTON.

www.ingramcontent.com/pod-product-compliance
Lightning Source LLC
Chambersburg PA
CBHW021550270326
41930CB00008B/1439

* 9 7 8 3 7 4 4 6 6 1 5 4 6 *